D1597352

THE CONCISE DICTIONARY OF DRESS

DICTI ONA RY

OF

DRESS

JUDITH CLARK & ADAM PHILLIPS

PHOTOGRAPHY BY

NORBERT SCHOERNER

Violette Editions
in association with Artangel

To Katherine Gieve and Gillian Brasse

First published in 2010 by Violette Editions,
an imprint of Violette Limited,
in association with Artangel

Violette Limited
1 Perham Road
London W14 9SR
www.violetteeditions.com
info@violetteeditions.com

Edited and produced by Robert Violette
Design and art direction by Studio Frith
Printed in Italy by Graphicom

Violette Editions would like to extend grateful thanks to everyone whose efforts
and enthusiasm have made the publication of this book possible: Judith Clark and Adam Phillips;
Norbert Schoerner and his production crew, Steve Langmanis, Hide Shimamura, Eric Young and
Stefan Krt; Frith Kerr and Amy Preston at Studio Frith; Tamsin Perrrett and Kate Burvill;
Rosalia D'Aprano and Graphicom; Michael Morris, Rob Bowman and Janette Scott at Artangel;
and, finally, the experts who gave such thought to challenging questions for Judith Clark.

ISBN 978-1-900828-35-2

A catalogue record for this book is available from the British Library.

Pages of this book are printed on recycled paper, made with 50–75%
post-consumer waste or are printed on certified virgin fibre
(FSC and/or other standard).

The Concise Dictionary of Dress, an Artangel commission by Judith Clark and Adam Phillips,
was held from 28 April to 27 June 2010 at Blythe House, 23 Blythe Road, London W14 0QX,
in collaboration with the Victoria and Albert Museum. Victoria and Albert Museum Blythe House is the
Museum's working store of its textiles, fashion, furniture, ceramics, glass, jewellery and fine arts collections.

Artangel is generously supported by Arts Council England and the private
patronage of the International Circle, Special Angels and The Company of Angels.
www.artangel.org.uk

CONTENTS

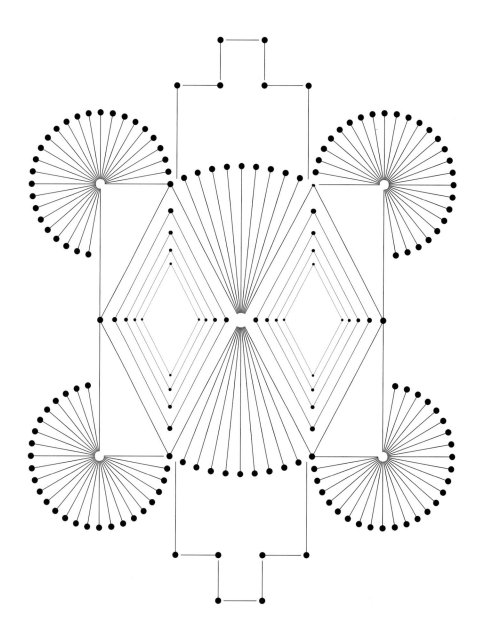

A
NOTE TO THE
READ
ER

This book, *The Concise Dictionary of Dress*, is based upon a site-specific project of the same name created by costume curator Judith Clark and psychoanalyst Adam Phillips. Artangel commissioned this collaboration, which took place in London from 28 April to 27 June 2010 at Blythe House, the Victoria & Albert Museum's working store for its art and design collections. This was the first occasion on which the V&A opened Blythe House to the public in this way. —————————— Clark and Phillips worked with the V&A and Artangel to create 11 installations on a tour through this vast building, from its rooftop to an underground coal bunker. Each of these installations was based upon words commonly associated with dress and for which Phillips has interpreted new definitions. This publication adds five further definitions of words not installed at Blythe House, as well as an introductory essay by Phillips, a series of questions posed anonymously to Judith Clark by experts in related fields and a detailed catalogue of the installation. Norbert Schoerner photographed the installation during overnight visits to Blythe House on 12 and 13 April. The definitions appear here in alphabetical order, though the journey through Blythe House took a different course. *Ed.*

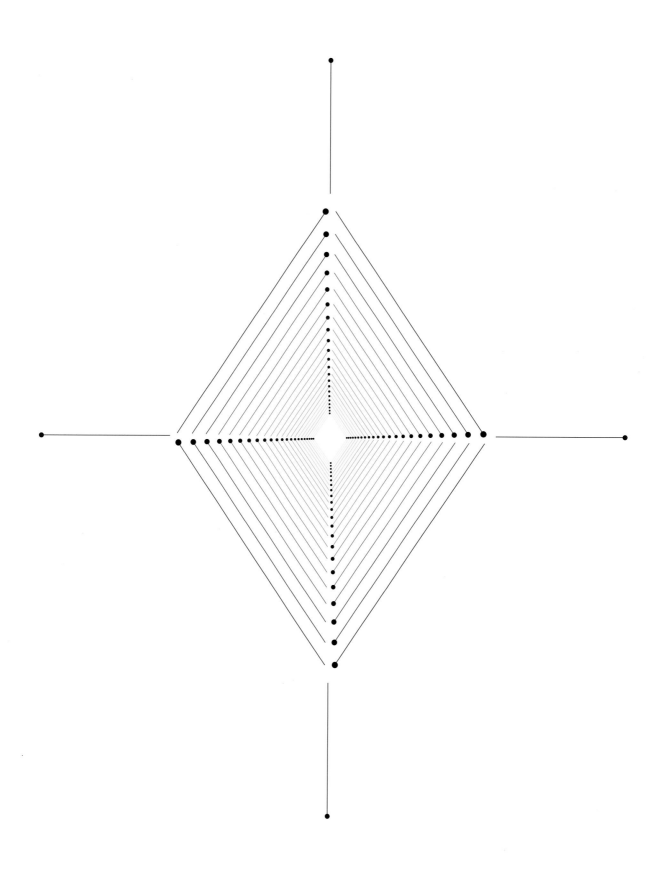

LOOK

IT

UP

BY

ADAM PHILLIPS

'ON
THE
CON
TRARY,
ETCETERA.
— I —
CON
CLUDED,
WE'LL
SEE WHAT
WE SHALL
SEE.'

SAUL BELLOW
HUMBOLDT'S GIFT

If you look up the word *consensus* in the dictionaries you will find that there is a consensus; 'agreement of various parts: agreement in opinion: unanimity' (*Chambers*); 'general or widespread agreement' (*Collins*); 'agreement' (*Shorter Oxford English Dictionary*). And if you look up the word *agreement*, the dictionaries go on agreeing with each other, but in doing so they bring more words into play. 'Concord: conformity: harmony: a compact, contract, treaty: an embellishment' (*Chambers*); '…the state of being of the same opinion; concord; harmony… the state of being similar or consistent; correspondence; conformity…' (*Collins*); 'the action of pleasing… consenting… atoning… a coming into accord; a mutual understanding; a covenant or treaty… mutual conformity of things, affinity…' (*SOED*). Definitions proliferate like family trees; genealogies are sets of competing directions. Every word in the dictionary sends you back to more words, but unlike any other book, every word in the dictionary is defined. So dictionaries, whatever else they are, are monuments to self-definition. They can tell you what they mean, unlike any other book. A dictionary is a self-describing artefact, if not a self-consuming one.

⸺⸺⸺⸺⸺⸺⸺ William Empson's 'general proposal' in his essay *Dictionaries* was 'that the interactions of the senses of a word should be included', but with the proviso that 'such a plan could be carried out without making the dictionary much longer'. Words also only make sense because their senses interact (*consensus* and *agreement* are irresistibly involved with each other); and dictionaries always threaten to get longer because someone is always having to decide where definition ends. And, indeed, what you need to know to use a dictionary (the audience may be potentially everyone who speaks the language, but you have to be literate to use it). You can't learn a language by using a dictionary, you can only use a dictionary once you have learnt the language (or enough of the language to use a dictionary). And to use a dictionary you need to know enough language for someone to explain to you how dictionaries work. People don't learn to use dictionaries by looking up the word *dictionary* in the dictionary. But if you do look up the word *dictionary* in the first great English dictionary, Samuel Johnson's *A Dictionary of the English Language* (1755), you find, 'A book containing the words of any language in alphabetical order, with explanations of their meaning; a lexicon; a vocabulary; a word-book'. This is the plainest, most eloquent common sense, and it asks us to wonder what it might be to explain the meaning of a word, and why a dictionary is more of a word-book than any other book? And, as this exhibition proposes, what it might be for a dictionary not to be a book, and not to be made only of words? —————————————————— All you get when you look up a word in the word-book dictionary is more words; and this makes dictionaries both exhaustive and inexhaustible. Like a maze or a labyrinth, we might wonder what gets us out of the dictionary once we get into it, and the answer is, the wish to use what we have learned, the reassurance provided by something that must know what it's talking about. After all, where else can you turn, apart from to other people, to find out what words mean and how to use them? To find this out, that is to say, in a systematic way, methodically? And if you don't trust the other people, where else can you turn – despite the fact that, like all books, the dictionary was actually written by more of these other people? We talk of putting our trust in God, or in scientists, but we don't talk of putting our trust in lexicographers. But if you were a new user of dictionaries, as a child is – as everyone was once, though the experience is always forgotten – you could easily feel that there is no way out of a dictionary because every definition might bring new words you have to look up. As adults, the way we use dictionaries helps us forget about this; ideally we just look the puzzling word up and carry on with what we are doing, which is going on using words as if we know what they mean. Only people who go to foreign countries carry dictionaries around with them. And dictionaries are, of course, books that no one ever reads from cover to cover, or in any sense reads through. Indeed one of the many strange things about dictionaries is that most of the words are never looked up; no one assumes that we just need dictionaries of difficult words. So dictionaries are all-or-nothing books, just-in-case books, that are used but mostly left unread, reassuring ways of storing words and their definitions whether or not we will ever need them. They are an insurance policy against possible misunderstanding. They reassure us that clarity and comprehension are available, that someone knows how to use every word. And even if they are maps for a country much of which we will never see – everyone sets limits to their vocabulary – we know that there is a map. As self-help books for speakers and readers and writers, they encourage us to go and try out their suggestions; they encourage our independence; they want us to use them when necessary, as a last resort. But they do believe in getting it right; they have standards – of accuracy, of probity, of economy – whether or not they set them. Lexicographers can't afford to be impressed by error, or enchanted by the misuse of words; or indeed by subversions of their genre. We don't want lexicographers to be like those philosophers whose method, in Gordon Baker's words, 'more often consists of taking note of possibilities to which one is blind than of establishing facts of which one is ignorant'. Despite the work of Ambrose Bierce, despite Flaubert's *Dictionary of Received Ideas* and George Bataille's contribution to the 'critical dictionary' in the 1920s, the dictionary has not been an improvisable form. We think of dictionaries as pragmatic rather than inspirational; they are supposed to be useable, not enchanting, books you are allowed to dip into, books you are not likely to discuss with other people (not much time is spent, for example, comparing dictionary definitions). After Johnson, whose *Dictionary* was a major cultural event – 'the world contemplated in wonder,' Boswell wrote, 'so stupendous a work achieved by one man,' referring to 'the great fame of his dictionary' – dictionaries have never been fashionable (though the mocking and manipulating and exposing of forms of classification seem to us now to have always been fashionable). The 18th century of Johnson's great *Dictionary* was also the great age of satire, but the dictionary quickly became a peculiarly staid cultural object. Though they are sometimes revered – the *Oxford English Dictionary* in particular – people are not irreverent about them. They are uncontroversial forms of authority, neither loved nor hated. Lots of people use them, and own them, but they are not popular. Unless you 'love words', whatever that means, the pleasures of the dictionary are limited. They tend to make us feel competent but not happy, right (or wrong) but not exhilarated. If dictionaries are not only useful, what else could they be? If dictionaries are good for storage, what good is storage, what kind of pleasure is it? The dictionary should for example show us why history and histories might matter, why the exhibiting of words might work for us; but this involves asking how words should be exhibited, how they might be most interestingly shown? And, as this exhibition suggests, why words alone may not always be a certain good, at least in dictionaries. As Empson remarks, 'How you are supposed to interpret what is put in a dictionary has been left extraordinarily obscure.' What is put in means what is kept out, and what is put together. And even when we read a dictionary we interpret and are supposed to. Dictionaries can only tell us what words mean by using them.

————————— What is kept out, and which words are allowed to associate with each other, is dictated by strictures of accuracy, a sense of language as exact, and exacting, as something that can be done properly. Dictionaries are never impolite. They are for people who want to get something right, or less wrong; for people who don't want things to be extraordinarily obscure. They are what people need in a certain kind of crisis. But then one of the striking things about dictionaries is how little they are used.

————————— Even though there are many words we are not quite sure about, only certain words ever get looked up in the dictionary (the words I have looked up in a dictionary in my life would be an odd kind of personal history). We might look up *consensus*, but we probably wouldn't look up *agreement*. So it is worth wondering what makes us do it, what the preconditions are for using the book; both what we want from it, and what we tend to get from it. We don't get, for example, definitions that we know off by heart; no one quotes dictionary definitions without the book or the definition in front of them. We want an accuracy from the dictionary but we come away with the gist, a better sense, a stronger impression; but we don't carry the definition with us exactly as we go on reading (by definition, a dictionary definition interrupts our reading). Learning a dictionary off by heart is not done. And how we actually use the definitions we acquire is more obscure than it might seem.

————————— We may think of a dictionary as a kind of tool kit, but we don't use what it provides with that kind of specificity; we get something helpful from the dictionary but there is a sense in which we have to forget the definition, or at least keep it in abeyance when we use the problematic word. Words are not tools in the sense that tools are. The situation – maybe the catastrophe – we are trying to avert is sometimes the *faux pas*, using the word in obviously the wrong way, and sometimes not being able to use the word to do what we want it to do; and sometimes not being able to use the word at all (the words we can never use might be like the clothes we can never wear). Dictionaries are for competence, for a kind of efficiency, for extending our verbal reach; they are not etiquette books, but they are supposed to improve our performance, to give us more of something we want. So when it comes to words and our using them, what is it that we want more of? If there is something excessive about dictionaries – they always run the risk, as Empson noted, of getting too long – there must be something excessive about what we want from them, or about what we imagine they can give us. Definitions, like habits, contain our excesses but can themselves be excessive.

Dictionaries always come with prefaces or introductions that help us to use them; indeed Johnson's preface to his monumental *A Dictionary of the English Language* is one of the essential starting points in the consideration of dictionaries in the English language. But what dictionaries essentially do is provide definitions; and by the same token they make us wonder about the definition as an object of desire, as something that we so much want that we have invented a particular genre of book that is full of them, that has – other than its prefaces and introductions, and explanatory notes – nothing but definitions in it.

What we want more of from dictionaries is definitions of individual words; and what dictionaries give us are first a re-description of the word in other words, the definition, and then, sometimes – a precedent definitively set by Johnson and continued in the *OED* – examples of historical usage. The word in other words, and examples of the word in sentences or phrases – in uses – from the past. So what is wanting more definitions, more definition, a wanting more of, and what do we want definitions to do for us, when definition itself is something that sets limits to excess? Why, in the self-fashioning called identity, is self-definition the thing? These are among the questions asked by this exhibition, which gives definitions of certain key words about dress and an object, an installation that defines the definition. Like looking up a word in a dictionary and finding a picture there instead of more words, it is not clear whether the word and its definition are the caption, or vice versa. It is like assuming that the word and its definition – the word and its accompanying installation – are mutually defining. There are no clothes without words about them; but some words can have clothes, material, about them. Words for clothes and clothes for words. Each with their respective histories. Clothes designers at their best, like lexicographers, are among the most remarkable historians in the culture, endlessly renewing an inheritance that is always fading, always going out of fashion.

●————————————— Definition can also depend upon a change of medium. Indeed, definition itself is redefined by a change of language. In this exhibition, the words and the objects illustrate each other. They bring out something in each other that they can't bring out by themselves. 'The definition of definition goes two ways, opposing,' AR Ammons writes in his poem *Essay on Poetics*, 'one direction cuts away, eliminating from relevance' but the other direction 'adds', 'recalls clusters'. Definition excludes – the irrelevant, the superfluous, the distracting; but it also includes – abundance, association, particularity.

●————————————— In this exhibition the definition of definition goes more than two ways, opposing and complementing and complicating and over-shadowing. If to define is always to set a limit – inclusion and exclusion, as Ammons intimates, always going together – then the idea of the limit, of the boundary, can itself be put in question. Boundaries only separate because they connect, like the clothes on a body. The privileged highlight the underprivileged. A foreground is a way of showing us a background. The words and the objects in the exhibition exhibit each other, show each other off. When Empson suggested that 'the interactions of the senses of a word should be included' in a dictionary, he was speaking up for the clashes and affinities of sense that words – and words and objects – work through. It is a picture of reciprocal animation, of joint enlivenings with unpredicted outcomes. It is difficult to imagine a dictionary divided against itself, sending itself up, making jokes and incongruous associations at its own expense, wanting to surprise us or even shock us. But if you let the interactions of the senses of a word be included, one of the things that can happen is that anything can happen. The fear of the lexicographer is that language never stops; the task of the lexicographer is to stop the task being infinite.

●————————————— So to play off, as this exhibition does, the making of dictionaries and the curating of dress is to go on combining words and objects, as we can't help but do, but in a different setting, a different context. One of things dramatised here is the connection, or otherwise between the commentary and the image, the writing (or speaking) about and the object. Promoting beauty over its detractors, and impurity over righteous indignation – 'idolatry and advertising, however, are indeed art, and the greatest works of art are inevitably a bit of both' – the great art-critic Dave Hickey makes a case for images and objects that might make us wary of dictionaries and their honest definitions. 'There are issues worth advancing in images', he writes in *The Invisible Dragon*, 'that are worth admiring – that the truth is never plain nor appearances sincere. To try to make them so is to neutralise the primary, gorgeous eccentricity of imagery in Western culture since the Reformation: the fact that it cannot be trusted, that images are always presumed to be proposing something contestable and controversial. This is the sheer, ebullient, slithering dangerous fun of it. No image is inviolable in our dance hall of visual politics. All images are potentially powerful. Bad graphics topple good governments and occlude good ideas. Good graphics sustain bad ideas and worse governments. The fluid nuancing of pleasure, power, and beauty is serious business in this culture.'

———————————— From a certain point of view, dictionaries could be seen to be neutralising the primary, gorgeous eccentricity of language (or trying to), making it plainer (and sincerer) than it ever could be. And certainly no one is going to be celebrating the primary, gorgeous eccentricity of a dictionary (Johnson acknowledges in the preface to his dictionary that 'such is the exuberance of signification which many words have obtained...it was scarcely possible to collect all their senses').

———————————— The installations in *The Concise Dictionary of Dress*, like the definitions of the key words, serve to loosen, or to set off in several directions, the issues worth advancing, which are very much to do with the idolatry of words and the advertising of dress (dress advertises the body, definitions pay tribute to the word). If imagery cannot be trusted – and dictionaries are trustworthy or they are nothing – and images (unlike words?) are 'always presumed to be proposing something contestable and controversial' (unlike dictionaries?), then words and images, words and material, are bound to set each other off. Whether we are being persuaded or seduced – persuaded because of ourselves, or persuaded in spite of ourselves – a dictionary of language and installation plays off information against evocation, getting it right against the gorgeous eccentricity of personal association. The difference between what you are told and what it makes you think, between what you see and what occurs to you; between what makes sense and what remains as undefined, unclear, indeterminate.

———————————— The psychoanalyst Ralph Greenson once suggested that it was better in the old days when little boys were dressed up as little girls to begin with, because at least it acknowledged that boys start by identifying with their mothers. The boy's first self-fashioning is as a boy-girl. These mothers who dressed their boys in dresses were not necessarily foisting a definition on their children, 'feminising' them, but acknowledging or co-operating with their self-definition. Greenson's paper, *Disidentifying from Mother*, made the simple point that the boy can only properly disidentify from his mother if he has first wholeheartedly both identified with her and been allowed to. The way the child dressed, or rather, the way the child was dressed, made this real.

————————— This, I think, is as much a point about definition as it is about gender; that just as you can only disidentify after you have identified – you can only be at all different by first being as much alike as possible – you can only undefine (or redefine) after you have defined (and there are, it is perhaps worth adding, the definitions born of attention, and the definitions born of inattention; a child is always the recipient of both, as is a word). A dictionary is not so much a text but a pre-text; its definitions are not orders or prescriptions but guidelines, jumping-off points. After all, what would it be like to talk or write like a dictionary? (No one says of a writer that she uses language with the accuracy of a dictionary.)

————————— Whatever the expressed intentions of lexicographers might be, a dictionary is a dressing-up box; it no more necessarily inspires uniform uses of language than laws inspire people to be well-behaved (on the contrary). We look up a word and then we can do something with it; we can, in a sense, apply it, but the definition doesn't work as an instruction (or a law). The dictionary is a source-book which gives us no inkling about how its words might be used – combined, defined, pronounced – in the future. Out of the definitions our indefinitions can come; not our misapplications, but our inevitable improvisations. And the dictionary is always evocative under the cover of being informative; we digest its definitions, we don't merely copy them. We identify with the explanation, then we go and use the word.

————————— Fashion, which aims for consensus while knowing that all consensus is provisional and precarious, is about the fact that things keep changing, that already existing materials can be remade into something new. Language keeps changing, but dictionaries stay the same (new dictionaries are few and far between, old dictionaries are infrequently revised). Just like the existing dictionaries of dress –

which are utterly reliant on illustration and technical description, and assume a straightforward correspondence between the image and its description – word-dictionaries have been conservative, in both senses, by nature. Archival rather than provocative, scholarly rather than intemperate, the traditional dictionary preserves traditions. And it does this partly by preserving the form of the dictionary itself.

————————————— But it is easy to forget that a definition is always, whatever else it is, the answer to a question; and that it is not always clear what the question is that any given definition supposedly answers. We may have assumed a too-limited repertoire for the dictionary; as though the dictionary, by definition, is a book we need to know where we are with (we don't want our lexicographers to start making things up, or moving things around, or making odd connections, or being vague or weird or tentative, or even suggestive: we don't want them to be poets; we don't want them to start answering questions we haven't asked them; we don't want them to write what-ever comes into their heads). But perhaps each of our languages needs a different kind, or different kinds, of dictionary; kinds that acknowledge the ways in which languages can outstrip the skills and methods of their lexicographers, kinds that give us a different picture of how a language might work; kinds that answer different questions about how to do things with words.

————————————— Clothes, another of our languages, another of our codes, another of the forms our histories take, keep changing, like words, but faster; and, like words, everybody uses them, and, whether they are conscious of it or not, everyone has their own style, just as everyone has their own vocabulary. The reason that people are disdainful of fashion is that they fear that many of the things they value most in their lives may be more like fashion than anything else. In this sense, dictionaries are always fighting a rearguard action; not against fashion, but against its inevitable excesses (it has to keep changing; it has to be something no one can keep track of). We have to imagine what a language would be like if it was like this. So there are no fashionable dictionaries (or indeed, fashionable definitions). And there can be no obvious dictionary for clothes, fashionable or otherwise, no straightforward reference book. *The Concise Dictionary of Dress* is, then, an unobvious dictionary; not a book, not made only out of words, but not without reference.

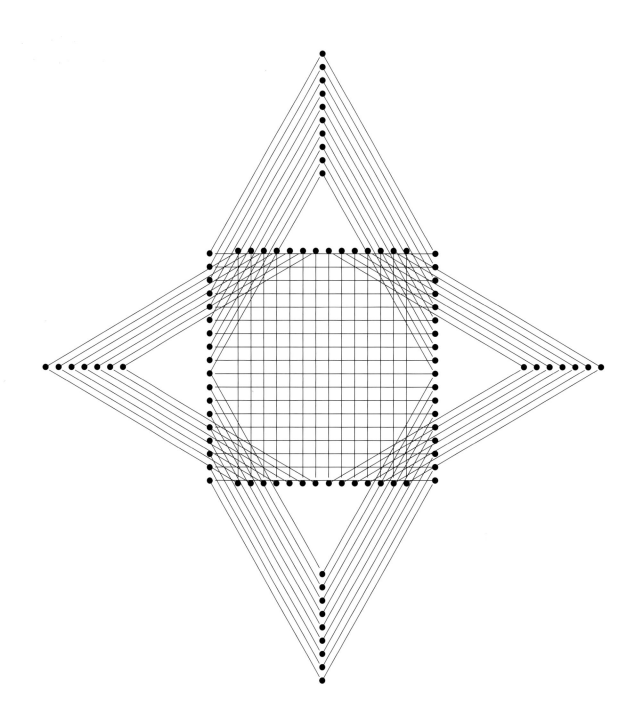

ARMOURED

BRASH

COMFORTABLE

CONFORMIST

CREASED

DIAPHANOUS

ESSENTIAL

FASHIONABLE

LOOSE

MEASURED

PLAIN

PRETENTIOUS

PROVOCATIVE

REVEALING

SHARP

TIGHT

ARMO
URE
D

1

Keeping a dark or secret profile.

2

Hardened for the elements; soft-centred.

3

Inviting attack by being prepared for it, provocative.

4

Heavier.

5

Sustaining belief in the inside and the outside,
the invulnerable space and the essentially unprotected body.

6

Clothes as noise.

7

Undressing revised.

BRA
S H

1

Unwitting courage; gusto; the enthusiasm of naïveté.

2

Careless of context, or blind to it.

3

Reckless self-exposure; unguarded self-promotion;
bumptious self-assertion; worn out.

4

Showing up and off the scandal of consensus,
the smug bond of shared embarrassments,
a space opened up that can only be closed.

5

Not worked into the pattern; obtrusive;
productive of unease and inner superiority,
and the unease of inner superiority.

6

The terrorism of the unashamed.

7

Confident; mistakable.

•————————————

[not installed at Blythe House]

TREATED

COMFO
RTAB
LE

1

A refuge; a nostalgia; the calm before or after.

2

The affluence of ease.

3

Fear of the future, rehearsed.

4

Pleasure as convenience; measured longing.

5

Space protected to forget that protection is required.

6

Invisibly armoured.

CONF
ORMI
ST

1

A state of essential simplification;
safe in numbers.

2

Recipient of an unnoticed demand,
complicit; choosing not to choose; compliant,
and therefore enraged; unwitting double agent.

3

Blended into a selected background.

4

Committed to difference, and by it;
horrified by the idiosyncrasy of desire;
uniformly agreeable.

5

Accurate, diligent; wired for surprise;
mourning variety.

6

Consensus as spell; idealist.

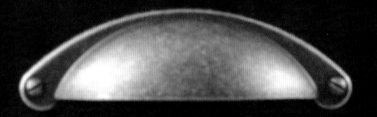

CREA
SE
D

1

The fold fixed.

2

The line designed by use.

3

Spread for conservation, sometimes with laughter.

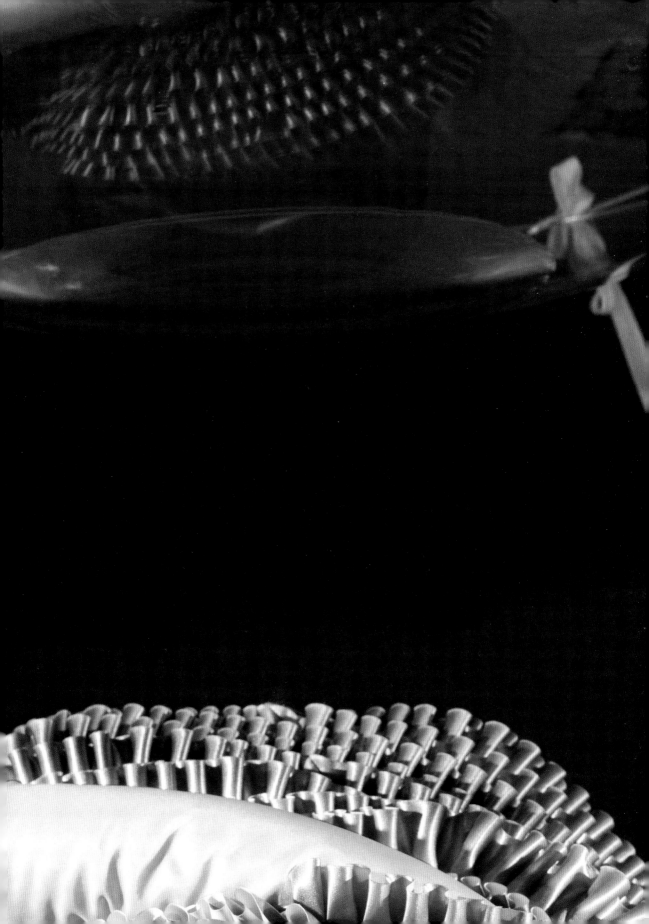

DIAPH
ANO
US

1

Seeing through as not seeing into; transparency as a veil.

2

The obstacle of clarity; invisible interruption.

3

The light layering of space.

[not installed at Blythe House]

ESSE
NTI
AL

1

Distracting.

2

Reduced to a, or the minimum;
pared down, spare, no more than itself.

3

A virtue made of a necessity, or vice versa.

4

Of exaggerated importance; privileged to avoid confusion,
fix attention, or encourage sacrifice.

5

That which quickens or concentrates a space;
the forcing of focus.

6

Exclusive; letting the trivial,
the irrelevant and the superfluous out of the bag.

7

More of the same.

8

Coercive, without aspect.

329) 330) Stylised life-size metal mannequins dressed in synthetic fabrics recline on "stages". (Photo Larkin.) — **331)** Display of fabrics which are sold by a Government-sponsored combine.

329) 330) Lebensgrosse abstrakte Metallfiguren auf „Bühnen" sind in Kunstfaserstoffe gekleidet. — **331)** Dekoration mit Stoffen, die von einem von der Regierung gemützten Kombinat verkauft werden.

329) 330) Figures textilliques plus grandes que nature, posées sur une escera » et venues de tissus synthétiques. — **331)** Etalage d'une entreprise textile controlée par l'Etat.

329

CELANESE Co. Ltd., London.
les. ∗ Textilien.

n / Entwurf / Décor: JEAN SAINT-MARTIN; ELIANE BONABEL

CELANESE Co. Ltd., London.
les. ∗ Textilien.

n / Entwurf / Décor: JEAN SAINT-MARTIN; ELIANE BONABEL

FASHI
ONAB
LE

1

A form of alarm; armour for the anticipated emergency;
secret knowledge of contemporary intimidations.

2

Excited impatience with the body;
something made to disappear;
anything that can be refashioned.

3

Of its time by promising a more alluring future;
a kick start, a longing, a private nostalgia.

4

History without footnotes; the past in new clothes;
undercover conservation.

5

Taking liberties on the future and parasitic on it.

6

Anything that tries to stop the present collapsing
back into the past; the new without fear.

7

Something that makes space for itself.

8

An experiment with pleasure,
without proof; living for the last moment.

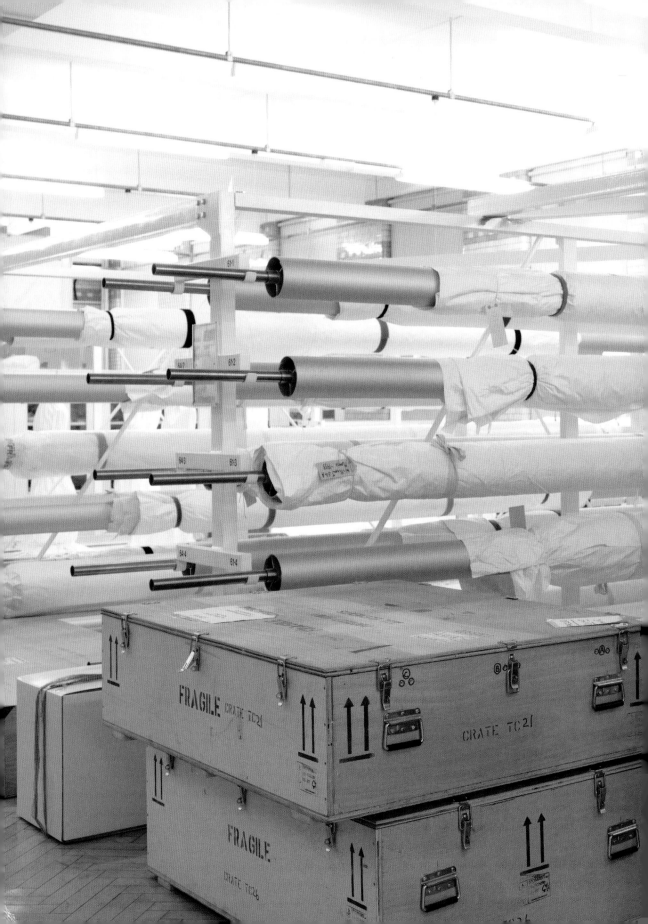

L O O
S E

1

Never knowingly over-attached; a disappearing act.

2

A moveable feast; not conforming to contour or arrangement;
subject to influence and gravity; seeking direction.

3

Of uncertain boundary.

MEAS
URE
D

1

Against chaos; a way of thinking about disarray;
calculated excess.

2

The fitted as fitting.

3

Proportion as the mother of virtue.

4

The milder ecstasies of the considered.

5

Contained by the idea of containment.

PLA
IN

1

Nothing special where nothing special intended.

2

Hiding to make room.

PRET
ENTI
OUS

1

Something pretending to be something that it is.

2

An experiment in excess; excess on trial.

3

The courting and claiming of ridicule; making
embarrassment the solution and not the problem.

4

Exposing a certain blandness in the environment,
a needless uniformity in the situation; a revealing
of assumptions; a reinforcing of conventions.

5

Full of misgiving.

23

PROVO
CATIV
E

1

Interested in other people.

2

The arousal of curiosity, curiosity as arousal;
showing off to discover what can be seen,
what can be shown, and what is showing;
quest for a more reflective, a more
interested mirror; the research of the shy.

3

Taking the stage, whatever; a drama out of a crisis.

4

Loss of faith in the audience; distrust of the evocative.

5

A composed tantrum.

[not installed at Blythe House]

REVE
ALI
NG

1

Concealing.

2

Knowing the other person's desire, or pretending to;
speaking on someone else's behalf.

3

The making of exciting assumptions.

4

Tantalising to avoid being tantalised;
using the body as a secret.

5

A confession of failure, a celebration of attention,
a knowing distraction.

6

A form of promising.

7

The performance of the unsustainable moment.

8

A telling mistake; an optical illusion.

9

Unavailing.

[not installed at Blythe House]

S H A

R P

1

Seeking access or good riddance; purposive;
suggesting a skill, a wound, a warning.

2

At the edge, or on it; not to be messed with, or up;
blunt about something; neat with a point.

3

Witty with menace.

4

Shafting the space; desire for the yielding,
the voluptuous; the nearly invisible.

5

Committed to the shield as weapon; painful.

6

Addressed.

[not installed at Blythe House]

T I G
H T

1

The holding in that is a holding out for something.

2

Restriction as exposure.

3

The triumph of continence.

4

Squeezed; mean; tensed; lithe; sleek; close; in readiness.

5

The intimate as threat and embrace;
the line between torture and comfort.

6

A gathering, a collecting, a smoothing over.

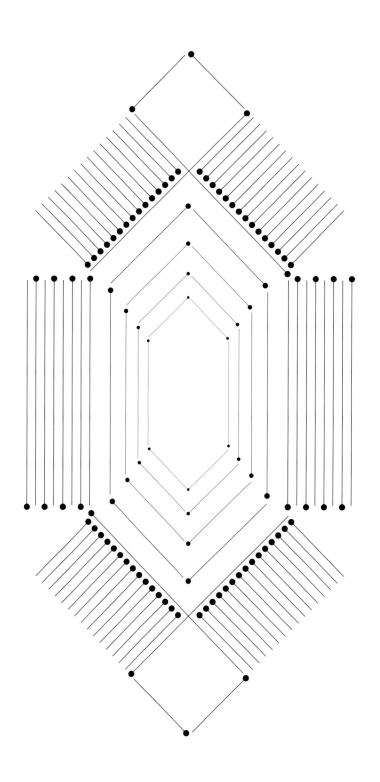

A

SERIES

OF

QUEST

IONS

ON

THE CONCISE DICTIONARY OF DRESS

POSED

ANON

YMOUSLY

TO

JUDITH CLARK

1

DOES ONE NEED
A BODY
TO BRING
A GARMENT
TO LIFE
AND WHY
?

This question is of course at the heart of curating dress, due to its inescapable relationship to the body. I suppose for me 'bringing to life' is not necessarily a priority – if by this we mean the re-enactment of history, or the proximity to its original use or look – but instead I use dress to talk about other things. (I am usually careful not to call myself a dress historian.)

In this particular series of installations there is a double loss of life, if you like: that of the garment without its body, and the garment out of sight, embedded within an archive. The archive is a very important ingredient here, as visitors do not expect garments to have been brought to life, but instead stored, classified and protected, and it is here that I am free to wonder: what are we storing when we are storing dress?

2

HOW DO
DEFINITIONS
BECOME
THREE-DIMENSIONAL
?

The project raises the issue of equivalences, of what text (or definition) goes with which dress and vice versa. They are mutually defining. People expect to see words in exhibitions, usually at the entrance, to the right of the door, and in a smaller font accompanying every object. When we 'look up' an object, it is with words that it is explained, rather than with other objects. Just as in dictionaries, the definitions, as Adam Phillips tells us here, are an 'insurance policy against possible misunderstanding'.

In 1999 I curated an exhibition called *Captions*, in the gallery I then ran. One dramatic catwalk ensemble by Alexander McQueen was installed and every visitor was asked to provide a caption, which was nailed to the wall of the gallery. It was the most overtly museological of the exhibitions I staged there. Had it been about defining the dress, I wonder how many of the captions might have made it into a dictionary?

I thought the definitions written by Adam would be freeing; and *against* the kind of information we expect from a consensually derived hierarchy of captions (date, place, material, etc.), that they would introduce re-descriptions and exciting misunderstandings; instead I have found myself treating the definitions as precisely as possible. In some cases I was rather obsessively attentive to the available connections.

One example is the installation paired with the word *measured*. The V&A has in its possession a white kid glove (*c.* 1800) that is decorated with a very finely printed diagonal grid into which dancing figures, flora and fauna are also printed. The figures, or minstrels, are reminiscent of engravings of late 16th-century/early 17th-century characters (*commedia* dell'arte's stock types) by Jacques Callot. Callot's architectural engravings are also held within the V&A prints and drawings collection. He was very preoccupied with representing depth of space and perspective. The V&A also holds ceramic figures that refer to his *commedia dell'arte* figures and also his studies of *gobbi* (hunchbacks). Information about one object might make you look up something else.

So, the object being questioned, or defined, I suppose, is the glove. I have designed a cabinet made up of many compartments: diamond-shaped, reflecting the visual compartmentalisation of the glove's decorative motif, which itself of course is a storage system of sorts, of imagery. Three diamond drawers are 'open', containing and revealing the glove and two miniature *gobbi* ceramic figures. The cabinet recedes dramatically, with raised sides to accentuate its perspective.

The glove itself could stand in for *measured*, mediated contact; it is measured (gloves fit like gloves – they are never too big nor too small), the pattern is meticulously measured, as are the scaled-down figures within it. There is mediated contact also with its subject, foreign to the wearer. The *gobbi* are about measured deviations from the ideal body and therefore draw attention to it, and so on. When this glove is stored, all these references are somehow stored within it, each contributing to its (3-D) definition.

3
HOW DOES
THE ARCHITECTURAL FORM

– THE FABRIC
AND SKIN OF
BLYTHE HOUSE,
WITH ITS VARIOUS
SECRET CHAMBERS
AND ELEGANT PROFILES,
CONCEALING/REVEALING
– EMBODY THE HUMAN FORM,
WHICH ONCE FILLED
AND ENLIVENED
THE DRESSES AND
PERSONAL ITEMS
?

The building or the exhibition's enfolding space is very important to this project, as it is in all my projects. Considerations around its particular qualities are often starting points. It might be too literal to create too many analogies between Blythe House and a body, but those that spring to mind about this project are those you suggest in the question, i.e. what is revealed and concealed: there is a very fine line between protection, conservation and the visibility of objects in the store, so what is considered particularly fragile is met with extra protection, etc. I suppose the installations ask what might be repressed in such a building.

One of the paradoxes of storage (secret chambers), for example, can be that no one gets pleasure from the stored objects. It is as though they refer to an always-deferred future when they might be exhibited, or re-exhibited. Stored objects are also stored moments of personal and cultural memory. Anxieties about exhibiting objects are anxieties about sharing them, about letting people come to their own conclusions about them.

I was careful to choose a variety of spaces, or alternative storage systems, within the project. It was necessary for the visitors to get a sense of the building and what was hidden from view as much as anything. The project could not have been restricted to one room, or one floor. There is a sense of camouflage as well, so the visitor feels that if they were to open any of the closed doors they might find another installation – another word.

4
DO YOU
BELIEVE IN
GHOSTS
?

I believe in what Italian stylist and jour-nalist Anna Piaggi calls the *animismo* (borrowed from the anthropological term *animism*) of an object. What she is referring to is not the essence of an object, but its afterlife, or rather the afterlife of the previous owner carried within an object. She can adopt a posture according to her knowledge of the previous owner of a dress. It is, for her, as powerful as the dress itself. I feel a bit like that about projects – that there are previous owners of the ideas that I might be incorporating. That references come with authors attached. Art historian Aby Warburg (mediated through Georges Didi-Huberman's research) haunts this project quite significantly. It is acted out, for example, in the first installation on the roof (the fact that the figure looks ghostly is less important). It alerts the visitor in an epigrammatic way that the concerns of the exhibition might be in 'air': air rendered

strong and expressive, air that has the capacity to make a gown billow out whilst on the other side revealing the contours of the body. For Warburg, this air is the 15th-century imaginary breeze that Huberman tells us Warburg elevated to the status of a 'cause', 'motive' or 'impetus' for a whole painting; that for 15th-century artists it became a tool for conveying pathos as well as being an essential accessory to a figure's corporeality. Curatorially there might be a way this could also be true. It might be what is extrinsic to the dress that is important. These issues have been pursued by curators of art, but not by dress historians. It also might be true that there are interesting differences around dress. If Warburg chose dress as expressive or as holding the expressiveness of the painting, then it might be worth considering his ideas in more detail for exhibitions of dress.

There is also a more literal reference to Aby Warburg in the project (in the word *essential*) and that is to his *Mnemosyne Atlas*. The series, which he described as 'an iconography of intervals' and 'art history without words', existed as black panels onto which he rehearsed the many restless visual connections between paintings and other examples (reproductions) of visual culture. Classical antiquity and its afterlife in High Renaissance art was his central preoccupation. For *essential*, I took photographs of the V&A plaster cast court, to which I have added James Laver's book *Style in Costume* (1949), commissioned a fake postage stamp featuring a famous Madeleine Vionnet dress, as more recent incarnations of the search for visual continuities. The new panels are placed around a commissioned stone carving of a recent classically draped Sophia Kokosalaki dress. *Essential* becomes essential, as in the afterlife of classicism, essential to the project (Warburg) and essential to my own past (I was brought up in a house opposite the Museum of Roman Civilisation in Rome, which houses the *other* plaster cast of Trajan's column, which I visited endlessly as a child).

There are also ghosts, of course, of the Post Office Savings Bank, of past curators, and their methodologies, of the objects and of all the uncurated exhibitions that the store might hold.

5
THERE SEEM
TO BE
TWO CATEGORIES
OF EMBODIMENT
IMPLIED BY
THE COMMISSION,
THE GHOST-LIKE
PRESENCE
OF CLOTHING
ONCE INHABITED
AND THE
ABSENT BODY
OF THE ARCHIVIST.
WHAT SORT
OF RELATIONSHIP BETWEEN
CURATOR AND CURATED
DO THESE
SHADOWS
AND VOIDS
SUGGEST
?

The installations invite the visitor to imagine the archivist or curator. They acknowledge intervention as part of interpretation.

In an extreme reversal there is one intervention where the 'real' dress is absent where the curator is present. The story is stored, the narrative is integral to the material. So here (in *plain*), a Balenciaga exhibition, for example, is stored as a rhythmic organisation of forms in space. A hypothetical exhibition – having hypothetically been staged – is then stored as a set of iconic gowns (now made up of shapes standing in for iconic Balenciaga gowns owned by the V&A). The exhibition is not dismembered. The spaces between the gowns have been stored in the same way as the gowns would be themselves, under white conservation-friendly Tyvek. The Tyvek creates therefore a holding pattern for an exhibition. The curator is gone but her intervention is recorded, not collapsed (as is the norm after an exhibition closes). Space is so fetishised in storage facilities that it would never occur to anyone to store space. But in storing it, I am proposing to store a curatorial project.

6
WHAT IS
MOST
INTERESTING:
FINDING,
COLLECTING,
DRAWING
OR
MAKING
THE EXHIBITION
?

Drawing exhibitions is what is most important to me, though it is not what is most
interesting to me. Drawing is always about
sketching and very rarely has dimensions
attached to it.

Coming across objects that I have an
appetite to look at and exhibit for reasons
that I never quite understand is exciting to
me. The glove (exhibited in MT5) was one of
the first objects I ever saw in the north store
(dress store) at the V&A when working in
the research department in 2002. Claire
Wilcox showed it to me and it stayed in my
mind, dormant, for the past eight years but
when I was shown it again I had remem-
bered it incredibly vividly. I browse archives,
I don't go in with an idea about what I am
looking for, but I do go in with an idea.
I didn't think – *measured* – that sounds
like a glove. I saw the glove and thought,
that is perfect for *measured*.

I start with objects, then often think
of patterns and then think of other objects
that will fit the pattern.

Even though I am not competent
enough physically to build a great part of
the exhibition, it is for me probably the most
interesting aspect of it. It *is* the exhibition.
This exhibition is an extreme version of this
as so much has been given to particularly
expert hands.

For *conformist*, I asked designer and
embroiderer Rosie Taylor-Davies to trans-
pose William Morris's design for the wall-
paper ('Windrush') onto a calico toile for
a medieval gown. I asked her to embroider
onto the garment the same section as Morris
had worked up in considerable detail in
paint into his grid.

It was about recording his methods
within a dress, about storing his loyalty
to ideals of craftsmanship within an idea
about taste so closely associated with the
V&A, it is revisiting what it is about him
that is worth storing. To store an ideal of
crafts-manship is to need to conform to it,
which Rosie has done in scrupulous detail –
that is making an exhibition: working it out
to that degree of detail.

7
IF I UNDERSTAND
CORRECTLY
THAT PART OF THE
CURATORIAL CONCEIT
OF THE EXHIBITION,
OR GUIDED WALK
THROUGH YOUR
CONCISE DICTIONARY OF DRESS,
OPERATES AT
THE NEXUS OF
TWO SYSTEMS OF STORAGE
– THE DICTIONARY FOR IDEAS
AND THE ARCHIVE FOR OBJECTS
– IS THE AMBITION OF STAGING
A BODILY ENCOUNTER
AT THIS NEXUS,
AS THE VIEWER IS TAKEN
THROUGH
BLYTHE HOUSE,
TO PRODUCE
A SENSE OF
RADICALLY UNSTABLE,
INDETERMINATE
OR UNDECIDABLE RELATION
BETWEEN THESE
SEMANTIC SYSTEMS
OR

IS IT RATHER
TO PROMPT
AN ENCOUNTER THAT
DE-SUBLIMATES THEIR
CULTURAL CONNECTIONS?
OR
IS IT THE IDEA
TO PRODUCE
SOMETHING LIKE
A CHIASMUS
– THE DRESSING OF
A DICTIONARY?
COULD THE DEFINITIONS
BE SUBSTITUTED,
SUCH THAT
CONFORMIST
IS NOW ASSOCIATED WITH
INTERVENTION VIII OF
THE FIVE ICONIC V&A GOWNS
OR
LOOSE ASSOCIATED WITH IV,
THE EIGHT WHITE
MANNEQUIN HEADS
?

There was a moment when Adam and I thought we might throw the definitions up in the air and 'pair' them up with installations blind. So your question is very pertinent. In a sense that would have been just as revealing a gesture as it would have illustrated (as I felt at that stage) that each described every one. That all dress functions in all the ways described or alluded to in all the written definitions. But in the more detailed stages of design, the specific connections became more important, and the details took over: we followed the idiosyncrasies of my selections. What I think now works is a lingering meaning from one to the next, that it is specific and cumulative at the same time. That definitions have things in common, even if just the fact of their ambivalence.

8
THE ARCHIVE OF
FASHION
HAS TRADITIONALLY BEEN
CONSTRUCTED AROUND
SURVIVING EXAMPLES OF
WOMEN'S DRESS.
THE CLOTHING
OF MEN
HAS PERHAPS
NOT SURVIVED
IN THE SAME QUANTITIES,
OR HAS NOT BEEN
PRIORITISED
AS IMPORTANT
OR INTERESTING.
IS IT SIGNIFICANT,
THEN,
THAT THE ONE ELEMENT
OF MALE DRESS
INCLUDED IN THE DICTIONARY
IS A SWORD
?

The choice was less about male dress and more about weaponry as an inadvertent storage for women's dress (in this case in the form of a Wedgwood plaque featuring a dancing nymph). I walked around Blythe House a great deal in preparation for this project and it was the instance that was most site-specific. The sword room, hung with hundreds of swords, looked like jewellery – like a category error. The issue was then to draw attention to this tiny plaque.

9

I'D LIKE JUDITH
TO INTERPRET
THE EPIGRAPH
BENJAMIN CHOSE FROM
LEOPARDI'S DIALOGUE
BETWEEN
FASHION AND DEATH:
'FASHION:
MR DEATH!
MR DEATH!'
(I NOTE THAT THE LATEST
TRANSLATION OF THE
BENJAMIN SUBSTITUTES
'MADAM' FOR 'MISTER',
BUT I CAN'T BELIEVE
THIS IS RIGHT.
MALE OR FEMALE,
I STILL NEED HELP.)

This dialogue is from Leopardi's *Operette Morali* (1827), between sisters Fashion and Death (both daughters of decay). They are competing over human frailty. Fashion triumphs over Death, bringing what is dead into the present.

It acknowledges modern cyclical fashion, which lives the paradox of being sustained by disappearances. Fashion is personified as sadistic and insatiable in 'opposition to the organic', to that which is natural. It convinces individuals to have what they do not need.

Walter Benjamin (1892–1940) used it as an epigraph in his *Arcades* project, at the beginning of the section *Grandville or the World Exhibition*. He was referring to the Universal Exhibition of 1867 – held in Paris at the height of the Second Empire – which was visited by 15 million people.

It is believed that 400,000 tickets were given to French industrial workers who had produced the spectacularised commodities in order to inspire aspirations to own them. Benjamin is talking about commodity fetishism, the power of which Grandville had turned into caricature.

10

WHERE IS
SPARTAN
AND
WHERE IS
SYBARITIC
HERE
?

It depends whether we are talking about taste (and in this case taste in dress) and the balance/conflict between the two extremes, or exhibition-making. One of the problems with extremes such as these in dress is that they become too literal to be suggestive, and become difficult to display. In fashion there is confusion added by a minimalist aesthetic – such as a perfectly cut little black dress – that became synonymous with extreme luxury. There is a sense in which exhibition design adopted this as well – the most expensive mannequins ever created, I believe, were those for the Armani show at the Guggenheim, where each was cut individually to disappear *totally* behind the contours of the dress. Getting rid of the body entirely, or rather its visible surrogate flesh. Its opposite tends to bow to the sexual excitement of catwalk shows, through over-styling, as though by extending the mannequin one is extending the sexual reach of the dress.

In this exhibition the terms apply more to the space in which it takes place. Blythe House is both spartan (the glazed-brick interiors and largely basic metal storage systems) and sybaritic – the thousands of objects stored within it and the fantasy of total excess and access that accompanies that knowledge.

11
WE TEND TO ASSUME THAT CLOTHES ARE FUNCTIONAL BUT IN TRUTH, THEY ARE FULL OF SLY (AND OFTEN BOLD) ALLUSIONS TO NONSENSE, DREAMING AND DESIRE. (THE RUFFLE. THE TIE. THE PATTERNED STOCKING.) IF CLOTHES ARE, ON SOME LEVEL, THE MANIFESTATION OF A COLLECTIVE REVERIE, WHAT DOES CONTEMPORARY FASHION REVEAL TO US ABOUT THE UNCONSCIOUS ASPIRATIONS OF LONDON IN THE EARLY 21ST CENTURY ?

I have often thought of what a functional exhibition might be, through a 'form follows function' kind of game. Whether you could ever truly derive one, decline one, and articulate it in a way that was grammatically correct. Through allusion you agree to lose your way, open yourself up to ridicule. You make a demand on the visitor, you invite a two-way conversation, just like bold clothes. Maybe it's about the fear of anonymity.

12
WHAT DOES THE DESIRABILITY OF HISTORIC/VINTAGE DRESS SAY ABOUT A PARTICULAR PERIOD IN TIME ?

It is impossible to know what is truly contemporary, so it is often described in terms of its affinities and differences with historic periods – it is easy with dress – which is why the *Dictionary* is an important organising idea for this project. It acknowledges that dress is just as taut-ological as dictionaries are: that in order to describe a dress you need more dresses, other objects. The word *fashionable* is organised around the idea of anachronism. I have used – as a motif – the moment when the V&A became associated with fashion rather than textiles and dress (1971), which many believe coincided with the staging of Beaton's *An Anthology of Fashion* that year. In the installation of *fashionable*, every head is dated 1971, whether retrieved from the past (a 1920s silver wig, a museum paper wig) or projected into a fashionable future. If an exhibition is fashionable, its subject becomes fashionable, and its subject is fashionable because it resonates with the time of its exhibition.

13
IN SHAKESPEARE'S
CYMBELINE,
THE INNOCENT IMOGEN,
LEARNING THAT HER HUSBAND
HAS ORDERED
HER MURDER,
THINKS OF HERSELF
AS AN EXPENSIVE,
CAST-OFF DRESS,
DESTINED TO BE
RIPPED AT THE SEAMS:
'POOR I AM STALE,
A GARMENT OUT OF FASHION,/
AND FOR I AM
RICHER THAN TO
HANG BY TH'WALLS/
I MUST BE RIPPED.
TO PIECES WITH ME!'
(III.IV.50-52).
THE UNDERLYING
EXPECTATION
IS THAT
THE RICHER
THE GARMENT,
THE MORE LIKELY IT IS,
WHEN IT GOES OUT OF FASHION,
TO BE RIPPED APART
AND REUSED.
WHAT DETERMINES
WHEN THIS PROCESS OF REUSE –
'TO PIECES WITH ME!'
– IS BROUGHT TO A
HALT
AND THE OBJECT IS
TAKEN OUT OF
CIRCULATION
'TO HANG BY TH'WALLS'
?

If a garment is valuable – should it go out of fashion and disappear or should it be material for something new? Should it be kept as *itself* – conserved in its original form or translated? Exhibitions are opportunities for translation, but as the question reveals there is always a murder, a death of the garment in synchronicity with its own time, according its own use. The museum is against recycling and *for* 'hanging by the walls' as soon as possible – in recent practice, as soon as the model takes off the gown at the end of the catwalk it is taken by the museum and preserved – it is preserved *before* it has had time to live. The more extreme and now more valuable contemporary gowns are commissioned by museums, bypassing even the body. Designed for exhibition, how much of the intention can be stored? If the context is interrupted, where is the line drawn around the garment?

14
HOW DOES
POLLUTION
FIGURE IN
YOUR UNDERSTANDING
OF THE MATERIALITY
AND TEMPORALITY
OF COSTUMES,
AND HOW YOU CURATE
THEIR EXHIBITION?
YOUR INTERVENTION IN THE
COAL BUNKER,
THE DIRTIEST ROOM,
SEEMS TO INVITE
THIS QUESTION,
AS DOES

YOUR TREATMENT
OF MORRIS,
WHO WAS FAMOUSLY
AGAINST
CLEANING BUILDINGS.
I AM THINKING OF
POLLUTION
BOTH IN THE
MODERN SENSE
OF ENVIRONMENTAL TOXICITY
AS IN THE
ARCHAIC SENSE
OF UNINTENTIONAL
BODILY SECRETIONS.
?

Foreign bodies are being brought into
Blythe House in the form of visitors, in a
sense that is the most controversial aspect
of the project. The negotiations around the
exhibition have been as interesting about
this question as the exhibition itself. Grant-
ing access, access to a stream of seven
bodies at a time, three times an hour into
Blythe House, as though this would put the
collection at risk. Every time the collection
is moved or handled it is considered at risk,
of accelerated decay and of accident.

    The coal bunker – most dirty, as you
point out, and constantly dripping water –
is like an intensified cycle of what is
expected to happen within the building
however fierce the conservation. On leaving
the controlled environment normal pollution,
damp and dirt feel all the more aggressive.
Creased is also linked to the feared fixed
folds in dress caused by the body's heat,
perspiration, and as the common site
of deterioration and therefore of focus.
The dress rests on a giant mattress, and
an oversized Perspex dish hung immediately
above the decorative frills catches the drips
from the damp ceiling dramatising the
process of protection from the environment.
The installation is ironic in that the fabric
of the silver dress *itself* has been treated
to withstand extreme weather conditions
(it was first shown on the catwalk under
a steady shower of rain).

15
IT IS
PLAIN
THAT WE,
AS CURATORS,
MEASURE FASHION
AGAINST TIME.
IS IT ALSO
ESSENTIAL
THAT WE SHOULD
ARMOUR OURSELVES
AGAINST
CONFORMITY
OF THINKING
?

If you find a way to distance curatorial
practice, or a methodology, by looking at
it from a different angle, or framing it,
you see it as time/culture-specific. Treating
a current curatorial consensus as time-
related is like putting something in inverted
commas – it becomes opinion, not natural.
I have placed a glass cabinet with a night-
gown on a stockman mannequin standing
in a large drawer in an oversized chest of
drawers. It means: this cabinet could be
stored as one of many ways of exhibiting
and looking after dress, it could be a
curatorial policy that has ceased to exist.

So the word *comfortable* – that could refer to the night-gown made by Paul Poiret for his wife Denise in 1910, is in fact referring to the cabinet in which it is stored.

One of my favorite short stories is *Tragedia di un Personaggio*, by Luigi Pirandello, first published in 1911. The protagonist, Dottor Fileno, uses what he describes as an inverted telescope – he looks through the large lens towards the smaller one – so that what is near (in time and space) appears far, far away in order that they may be better reflected upon.

'*In somma, di quel suo metodo il dottor Fileno s'era fatto come un cannocchiale. Lo apriva, ma non si metteva già a guardare verso l'avvenire, dove sapeva che non avrebbe veduto nulla; persuadeva l'anima sua a esser contenta di porsi a mirare dalla lente più grande, volta l'avvenire, attraverso la piccola, appuntata al presente. E la sua anima così guardava col cannocchiale rivoltato, e il presente subito le s'impiccioliva, lontano lontano. Il dottor Fileno attendava da varii anni a comporre un libro, che avrebbe fatto epoca certamente. Il libro aveva appunto per tiolo La filosofia del lontano.*'*

['In short, Dr Fileno has made a sort of telescope for himself out of that method of his. He would open it, but now not with the intention of looking toward the future, where he knew he would see nothing. He convinced his mind that it should be contented to look through the larger lens, which was pointed at the future, toward the smaller one, which was pointed at the present. And so his mind looked through the 'wrong' end of the telescope, and immediately the present became very small and distant. Dr Fileno had been looking forward for several years to writing a book that would certainly create a stir. And, in fact, the title of the book was *The Philosophy of Distance*.']

*Luigi Pirandello, 'La Tragedia di un Personaggio', *Corriere della Sera*, 19 October 1911 (trans. and ed. Stanley Applebaum, 'A Character's Tragedy', in *Eleven Short Stories*, New York: Dover, 1994).

THE
QUES
TION
ERS

Rebecca Arnold is Oak Foundation Lecturer in History of Dress and Textiles at the Courtauld Institute of Art, London.

Yuri Avvakumov has designed about 50 exhibitions as an architect, taken part in about 500 as an artist and organized about 50 as a curator.

Judith Blackall is Head of Artistic Programmes at the Museum of Contemporary Art, Sydney.

Christopher Breward is Head of Research at the Victoria & Albert Museum and a widely published author on the history and culture of fashion.

Timothy James Clark holds the George C. and Helen N. Pardee Chair as Professor of Modern Art at the University of California, Berkeley.

Kaat Debo joined MoMu, Antwerp's Fashion Museum, after studying literature at the Universities of Antwerp and Berlin. From 2001 to the present she has been responsible for the museum's exhibitions policy and has curated several of its shows. In 2009 she became director of the museum. She regularly lectures and writes on contemporary fashion.

Caroline Evans is Professor of Fashion History and Theory, Central Saint Martins College of Art and Design.

Stephen Greenblatt is a professor of English at Harvard University and the author of many books, including *Will in the World: How Shakespeare Became Shakespeare* (Norton, 2004).

Jennifer Higgie is co-editor of *frieze*.

Jorge Otero-Pailos is an architect, artist and theorist specialized in experimental forms of preservation. His installations have been exhibited in major international shows including the Venice Art Biennale (2009) and Manifesta 7 (2008). He is the Founder and Editor of *Future Anterior* and the author of *Architecture's Historical Turn: Phenomenology and the Rise of the Postmodern* (University of Minnesota Press, 2010).

Andrew Sant is an English-born Australian poet whose most recent book is *Fuel* (Black Pepper, 2009).

Felicity D. Scott is Director of the programme in Critical, Curatorial and Conceptual Practices at the Graduate School of Architecture, Planning and Preservation, Columbia University, and a founding co-editor of *Grey Room*, a quarterly journal of architecture, art, media and politics published by MIT Press since Autumn 2000.

Calum Storrie is an exhibition designer and writer. He lives on the Balls Pond Road in London.

Claire Wilcox is Senior Curator of Fashion at the Victoria & Albert Museum. She created *Fashion in Motion* (1999–2010) and her exhibitions include *Radical Fashion* (2001), *Versace at the V&A* (2002), *Vivienne Westwood* (2004) and *The Golden Age of Couture* (2007).

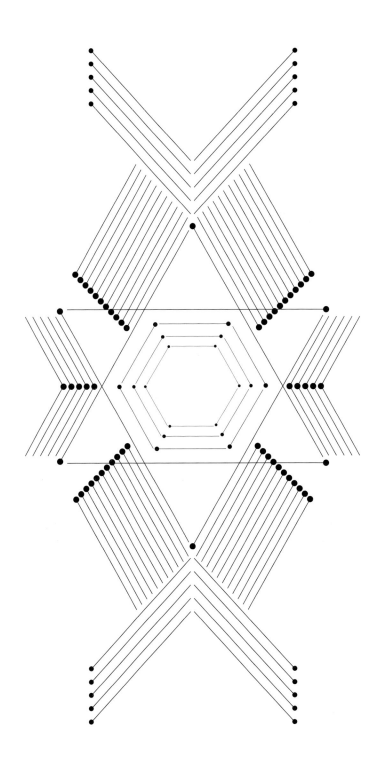

A

CATALOGUE

OF

WORKS

APPEARING

IN THE INSTALLATION

OF

THE CONCISE DICTIONARY OF DRESS

AT

BLYTHE

HOUSE

LONDON

28 APRIL TO 27 JUNE 2010

ARMOURED

COMFORTABLE

CONFORMIST

CREASED

ESSENTIAL

FASHIONABLE

LOOSE

MEASURED

PLAIN

PRETENTIOUS

TIGHT

Catalogue entries for each definition installed at Blythe House provide the location of the works, as well as reference information and illustrations. Original preliminary sketches are by Judith Clark, and all photography by Norbert Schoerner, unless otherwise stated.

ARMOURED

Pages: 22 to 28
Location: Rooftop sentinel (Blythe House exterior)
Work installed: *Breeze*, made by Simon Ings, 2010, resin cast, designed and commissioned by Judith Clark.

Reference: *The Act Directs*, fashion plate by Niklaus von Heideloff (1761–1832), from *Gallery of Fashion*, vol. IV (London: Heideloff at Gallery of Fashion, 1797), hand-coloured print on paper, 30.5 x 24 cm, Victoria and Albert Museum no. L.256-1943 (RC R 14) © V&A Images/Victoria and Albert Museum, London.

COMFORTABLE

Pages: 30 to 35
Location: Fourth floor furniture store, rolling racks (Blythe House room FF15)
Work installed: Madame Poiret's night gown, by Paul Poiret (1879–1944), 1910, white linen, courtesy Martin Kamer.

Reference: Photograph of a cabinet housing historical vestments and copes installed on the 'Bridge' Galleries surrounding the main entrance and dome at the Victoria and Albert Museum, from the *Photographic Guardbooks*, unknown photographer, 1920, museum negative 49414 © V&A Images/Victoria and Albert Museum, London.

CONFORMIST

Pages: 36 to 41
Location: Fourth floor furniture store, rolling racks
(Blythe House room FF15)
Work installed: *Windrush*, made by Rosie Taylor-
Davies, 2010, silk embroidered on calico toile dress,
giclée print, pencil and watercolour on paper,
200 x 290 cm, designed and commissioned by
Judith Clark. The William Morris dress was drawn
by hand in HB pencil on calico mounted into a 61 cm
wooden embroidery slate frame, then painted with
Setasilk fabric paint and Seidenmalerei Javana
silk paint. The larger motifs in the foreground were
then traced onto silk metal organza that had been
backed with powerwoven Dupion silk fabric and
applied to the calico. Further embellishment of the
design was worked in coloured stranded silk thread
and a variety of metal threads. The small leaves
were worked in Pearl Cotton. The veins and stems
were worked in Pearl Purl metal thread of varying
colours and metal types including one that has a
2% gold content. Metal spangles were applied to
the centres of some of the flowers and to the strap
work. The three-dimensional leaves were worked
in a separate ring frame in coloured stranded
silk thread onto metal silk organza backed with
powerwoven Dupion silk and then applied to the

main frame. The edges of the three-dimensional
leaves were worked in 2% gold metal Pearl Purl.
The metal threads were couched with waxed
spun polyester thread. Copper metal thread was
used to work further detail into the strap work.
The embroidery took 354 hours.

Reference: 'Windrush' pattern by William Morris
(1834–96), *c.*1883, pencil and watercolour,
131.5 x 99.6 cm, courtesy The William Morris Society
at Kelmscott House.

CREASED

Pages: 42 to 49
Location: Basement, coal bunker
(Blythe House outbuildings)

Works installed: 1 Dress by Junya Watanabe for Comme des Garçons, Autumn/Winter 1999, fabric created by Toray to withstand extreme weather conditions (originally shown by Comme des Garçons under a constant shower of rain), private collection. **2** *Conservation Pillow*, made by Sam Collins, 2010, foam, canvas and linen, 300 x 280 x 100 cm, designed and commmissioned by Judith Clark.

Reference: The new Textile Conservation Studio at the Victoria and Albert Museum, by V&A Photographic Studio © V&A Images/Victoria and Albert Museum, London.

ESSENTIAL

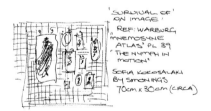

Pages: 51 to 57
Location: Third floor mezzanine, sculpture store (Blythe House room MT6)

Works installed: clockwise from far left:
1 Photograph of *Lot's Wife*, by William Hamo Thornycroft (1850–1925), 1877–78, marble, h. 193 cm, on loan to the V&A sculpture collection from Leighton House, by Judith Clark, 2010.
2 Photograph of *Pandora*, by John Gibson (1790–1866), c. 1860, marble, h. 173 cm, given by Mrs Penn, Victoria and Albert Museum no. A-3-1922, by Judith Clark, 2010. **3** Photocopy of *Una and the Wood Nymphs after W E Frost, ARA*, by Caldesi & Montecchi (active 1850s), 1857–58, Victoria and Albert Museum no. 34:436.
4 Necklace pendant with Wedgwood jasperware, 1884, by K T Jewel, 2008. **5** *Vionnet* postage stamp, made by Alice Smith, 2010, designed and commissioned by Judith Clark. **6–7** Plaster cast relief of water nymphs and putti from the *Fontaine des Innocents*, by Jean Goujon (c. 1510–65), sculpted 1547–49, cast 1882 (Paris), plaster of Paris, 229 x 61.5 cm, Victoria and Albert Museum no. REPRO.1882-5. **8–9**, *International Window Display*, ed. Walter Herdeg (London: Cassell, 1951) pp. 51 and 226. **10** *Style in Costume*, by James Laver (London: Oxford University Press, 1949). **11** *The Concise History of Costume and Fashion*, by James Laver (London: Macmillan, 1980).
12 Photograph of *Monument to Emily Georgiana, Countess of Winchilsea*, by Lawrence Macdonald (1799–1866), signed and dated 1850, marble, 89.9 x 55.9 x 135.6 cm, Victoria and Albert Museum no. A.188-1969, by Judith Clark, 2010. **13** Panel 5 of the *Mnemosyne Atlas*, by Aby Warburg, from *Aby Warburg and The Image in Motion*, by Philippe-Alain Michaud, et al. (New York: Zone Books, 2004), p. 11. **14** Stone carving of Sofia Kokosalaki 2006 dress, made by Simon Ings, 2010, Lapenne stone, 70 x 40 cm, designed and commissioned by Judith Clark.

Reference: *Mnemosyne Atlas*, by Aby Warburg (1866–1929), 1924–29, courtesy The Warburg Institute (illustrated overleaf).

FASHIONABLE

GLASS
FRONTED
DRESS
GALL.
CABINET.

WIGS x10
"1971"

Pages: 58 to 65

Location: Third floor, textile store cabinet
(Blythe House room T6)

Works installed: 1 Feather wig, made by Judith
Clark, 2010. **2** Paper wig, made by Judith Clark,
2010. **3** Beaded wig in the style of a 1930s hairstyle,
made by Rosie Taylor-Davies, 2010, synthetic Nymo
thread, plastic sequins, two cut sol gel satin 2mm
beads, cotton sheeting, polyester felt, wool felt,
100% spun polyester thread, antique beads,
plastic coated pearls, glass beads, designed and
commissioned by Judith Clark. **4** *1971 hair*,
made by Justin Smith Esquire, 2010, designed and
commissioned by Judith Clark. **5** Silver wire cocktail
wig, maker unknown, late 1920s, courtesy Sheila
Cook textiles (illustrated right). **6** Collar, designed by
Walter van Bierendonck, 2003. **7** Knitted hood, after
Cecil Beaton, made by Julia Billbäck, 2010, 100%
acrylic, designed and commissioned by Judith Clark.
8 Chrome head, by Proportion, 2010.

LOOSE

SWORDS
ROOM

SPOT LIT
"DRESS
SWORD"
+
BUCKLES
UR
FOB
(WEDGEWOOD)
ON
SUPPORT

Pages: 66 to 72

Location: Ground floor mezzanine, sword store
(Blythe House room MG5)

Works installed: 1 Sword-hilt, cut steel by Matthew
Boulton, set with Jasperware plaques by Josiah
Wedgwood and Sons Ltd, c. 1790, hilt 16.5 cm,
blade 83 x 10 x 8 cm, Victoria and Albert Museum
no. 1735-1888. **2** Buckle, one of a pair, cut steel,
possibly by Matthew Boulton, mounted with Jasperware plaques by Josiah Wedgwood and Sons Ltd,
1776-1820, steel, jasperware, 8.6 x 7.9 x 3 cm,
Pfungst Reavil Bequest, Victoria and Albert
Museum no. M.2-1969 (illustrated right, © V&A
Images/Victoria and Albert Museum, London).

Reference: Engraving, *Coup de bouton* caricature for the fashion for cut steel, artist unknown, 1777, published by W Humphrey of Gerrard Street, Soho; re-published in *The Journal of the Antique Metalware Society*, vol. 17, June 2009, Library of Congress no. LC-USZ62-52096.

MEASURED

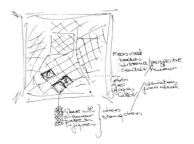

Pages: 73 to 79
Location: Third floor mezzanine, tank cupboard, (Blythe House room MT5)
Works installed: 1 Glove, maker unknown, *c.* 1800, France, kid leather, linen thread, printed with hand sewing, 22.5 x 9 cm and 22.5 x 8.5 cm, given by Mrs C J Wallace, Victoria and Albert Museum no. T.169&A–1922 (illustrated overleaf, © V&A Images /Victoria and Albert Museum, London). **2** Glazed porcelain figurine, hunchback dwarf musician playing the bagpipes, from the troupe Les Gobbis, maker unknown, 19th century, France, 9.5 x 4 cm, base 1 x 4.1 x 4.2 cm, bequest of Robert Eddison, accepted by HM Government in lieu of Inheritance Tax and allocated to the Victoria and Albert Museum, 1996, Museum no. S.1015-1996. **3** Glazed porcelain figurine, hunchback dwarf musician playing a hurdy gurdy, from the troupe Les Gobbis, maker unknown, 19th century, France, 9.5 x 4 cm, base 0.9 x 4.3 x 4 cm, bequest of Robert Eddison, accepted by HM Government in lieu of Inheritance Tax and allocated to the Victoria and Albert Museum, 1996, Museum no. S.1011-1996 (illustrated overleaf, © V&A Images/Victoria and Albert Museum, London).

Reference: Print, *Interior of a Palace*, possibly an etching by Jacques Callot (1592–1635), 17th century, paper, ink, 26.4 x 33.7 cm (print size), Harry Beard Collection, Victoria and Albert Museum no. S1838-2009 © V&A Images /Victoria and Albert Museum, London.

PLAIN

Pages: 80 to 85
Location: Third floor, textile store
(Blythe House room T6)
Work installed: *Balenciaga: A Retrospective*, made by Rosie Taylor-Davies, 2010, Tyvek, crinoline, Pelmet Vilene, cotton tape, card, bubble wrap, PVC tubing, designed and commissioned by Judith Clark.

Reference: Short evening dress (*robe du soir courte*), Cristóbal Balenciaga (1895–1972), Autumn/Winter 1958, Paris, black lace over black crêpe de Chine underdress with satin bows, Victoria and Albert Museum no. T.334–1997 © V&A Images/Victoria and Albert Museum, London.

PRETENTIOUS

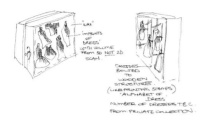

Pages: 86 to 96
Location: Fourth floor furniture store, rolling racks
(Blythe House room FF15)
Works installed: 1 Cocktail dress, labelled Chanel
c. 1922, crystal embroidered, yellow pan velvet,
courtesy Martin Kamer. **2** Dancing dress, by
Madeleine Vionnet, *c.* 1918, not labelled, black silk
charmeuse tassel trim, courtesy Martin Kamer.
3 *Goddess* evening gown, labelled Grès, *c.* 1960,
white silk chiffon; evening belt made for Madame
Grès, possibly Lallane *c.* 1960, gold metal, courtesy
Martin Kamer. **4** Cocktail dress with slip and belt,
by Madeleine Vionnet, *c.* 1925, black silk over cher
silk charmeuse, courtesy Martin Kamer. **5** *Rose*
paper dress by Harry Gordon, 1968, paper (75%
rayon, 25% nylon), screenprinted, courtesy Junnaa
Wroblewski. **6** Evening cape made from 'Roses
Grandes' fabric used by Paul Poiret, *c.* 1922, gold
lamé on black silk, courtesy Martin Kamer. **7** *Black
Rose*, by Charlie Le Mindu, 'Religion sex bullshit
lucifer' collection, Autumn/Winter 2010, styrene
plastic covered with black acrylic paint, with nylon
ribbon in the base, courtesy Charlie Le Mindu.
8 Cocktail dress, by Lanvin, June 1926, published in
Art, Gout & Beauté (Paris, 1926), not labelled, black
silk taffeta, courtesy Martin Kamer. **9** *Making an
Impression*, wax imprints of dresses, made by Simon
Ings, 2010, wax, 290 x 546 cm, commissioned for
this installation by Judith Clark.

Reference: Plaster mould for a wax relief of
The Marquess of Stafford, by Catherine Andras
(1775–1860), *c.* 1800, England, plaster of Paris,
17.5 cm, bequest of Rupert Gunnis, Victoria and
Albert Museum no. A.118 to 123–1965 © V&A Images
/Victoria and Albert Museum, London.

TIGHT

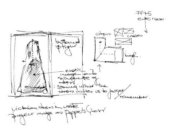

Pages: 102 to 107
Location: Fourth floor, larder
(Blythe House room FF45)
Works installed: 1 Erotic photograph, photographer
unknown, 1855, collection Uwe Scheid. **2** Victorian
suit, maker unknown, *c.* 1865, private collection.

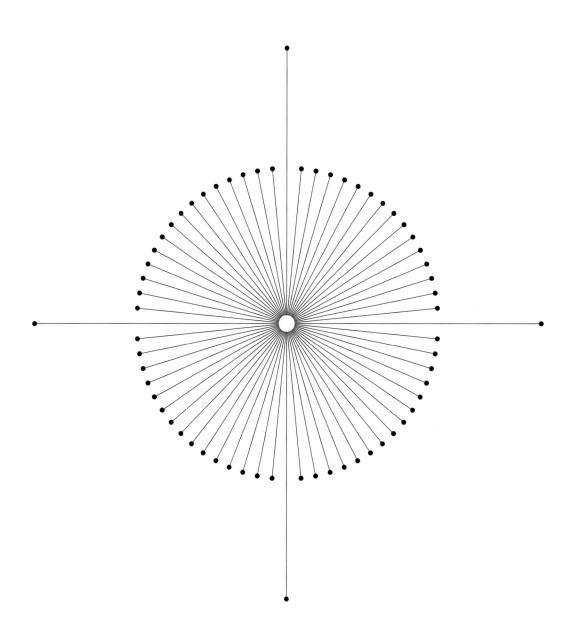

A F T E R

WORD

BY

MICHAEL MORRIS

CO-DIRECTOR, ARTANGEL

The *Dictionary of Dress* came about over several years through a meandering meeting of minds. It was finally made *Concise* thanks in part to the compelling constraints of its location: a working store of conserved artefacts into which Judith Clark and Adam Phillips introduced a thread of words. In this way, during the spring of 2010, the Blythe House depot briefly became a dictionary, each stored word defined and displayed through a fluid interconnection of language, image, history and place.

The chosen words and their imagined definitions reflect on how clothes function as a cover-up for what might lie beneath: the feelings and desires that need masking; the hidden wounds that must be dressed; the way in which what is worn defines yet defends the wearer – a dress code designed both to conceal and reveal.

In the labyrinthine zones and passages of Blythe House, our thread of words became a walking trail of discovery begun in a goods lift and concluded in a coal bunker. It was a dictionary you could visit. In the form of this book, the words are called to order and re-presented alphabetically and photographically, regulated as all illustrated dictionaries must be.

Measureless thanks are due to Judith Clark and Adam Phillips for conceiving *The Concise Dictionary of Dress* and entrusting its incubation and delivery to Artangel. For allowing the project such a perfect home, we are indebted to the commitment and support throughout of Sir Mark Jones, Moira Gemmill and Damien

Whitmore at the V&A as well as to a great many of the museum staff who helped us navigate the delicacies of making interventions within a working archive. In this regard, particular thanks are due to Lauren Parker, Jana Scholze, Sarah Terkaoui and Edwina Ehrman. And to Professor Frances Corner at the London College of Fashion, enthusiastic and supportive from the outset. For always being with us on the journey and usually the first to identify short cuts, very special thanks to Glenn Benson whose enthusiasm embodies the Blythe spirit that enabled Artangel's production team – purposefully led by Rob Bowman and Sam Collins, with the valued help of Sofia Hedman – to construct and install the displayed definitions.

Finally, I'd like to thank publisher Robert Violette, photographer Norbert Schoerner and designer Frith Kerr for conceiving of such a beautiful and enduring way to store the words chosen and the images made.